THE USBORNE
Impressionists Sticker Book

Sarah Courtauld & Kate Davies

Illustrated by Shirley Chiang

Designed by Nicola Butler   Edited by Jane Chisholm   Consultant: Kathy Adler

CONTENTS

Published in association with
National Gallery Company Limited

WHO WERE THE IMPRESSIONISTS?

In the late 19th century, a group of young artists living in France started painting in a bold new way. Here are some of the artists who became known as the Impressionists.

SELF PORTRAIT WITH A BERET
1886
Claude-Oscar Monet

Claude-Oscar Monet was a young artist living in Paris who was inspired by painting nature. In 1874, he and his friends put on an exhibition of their paintings. One of Monet's paintings was called *Impression, Sunrise*.

IMPRESSION, SUNRISE
1872
Claude-Oscar Monet

Many people hated the exhibition Monet and his friends organized, because they didn't understand the paintings. One critic called Monet an 'impressionist', because he thought this painting looked like a messy sketch. Soon, the artists became known as the 'Impressionists'.

SELF PORTRAIT
About 1873
Camille Pissarro

"This painting is less finished than a wallpaper design!"

An art critic

Camille Pissarro painted landscapes and scenes of his local town. The Impressionists put on eight exhibitions, and Pissarro showed his paintings in all of them.

Pierre-Auguste Renoir studied art with his friend Monet. He painted bright, sunlit pictures of people enjoying themselves.

SELF PORTRAIT
About 1875
Pierre-Auguste Renoir

Edouard Manet was older than the Impressionists, and he didn't show his paintings in the Impressionist exhibitions, but he often met up with Monet, Degas and other artists to talk about art.

DETAIL OF MANET FROM MUSIC IN THE TUILERIES GARDENS
1862
Edouard Manet

BERTHE MORISOT WITH A BOUQUET OF VIOLETS
1872
Edouard Manet

Berthe Morisot was an artist and a friend of Manet's. He once gave her an easel as a Christmas present.

Most people didn't take women artists seriously in her day, but Morisot is now regarded as a great Impressionist painter. She painted lots of scenes of family life.

Many of the Impressionists liked painting in the countryside, but Edgar Degas preferred painting dancers and scenes of Paris nightlife. He even joked that the police should shoot anyone who painted outside.

SELF PORTRAIT
About 1862
Edgar Degas

The other artists in the group included Alfred Sisley, Gustave Caillebotte (who bought lots of the Impressionists' paintings, too) and Mary Cassatt, an American living in Paris.

SELF PORTRAIT
About 1880
Mary Cassatt

Gustave Caillebotte

Alfred Sisley

PAINTING OUTDOORS

The Impressionists often painted outdoors to capture the changing effects of sunlight. New oil paints had been invented, and they were sold in tubes, which made them easier to carry on painting expeditions.

Before paint tubes were invented, paints were stored in leaky pigs' bladders. The new metal paint tubes made it easier for artists to pack up their paints and take them on trips.

Artists carried their paints in a wooden box, along with a palette to mix them on.

Monet painted this scene in the village where he lived. He took a hot water bottle with him to keep him warm. Once he stayed out in the snow so long that he got icicles in his beard.

SNOW SCENE AT ARGENTEUIL
1875
Claude-Oscar Monet

Monet was so interested in the effects of changing light that he painted twenty five canvases of grainstacks at different times of day, and different times of the year.

Pissarro couldn't paint outside because he had eye problems and had to avoid getting dust in his eyes. He painted this snowy scene of Paris from a hotel window instead.

GRAINSTACKS, SUNSET
1891
Claude-Oscar Monet

THE LOUVRE UNDER SNOW
1902
Camille Pissarro

Sisley moved from Paris to the country in 1880, because he was too poor to stay in the city. But this turned out to be good for his career. The paintings he did in the fresh country air were brighter, and more popular.

Alfred Sisley

"Every painting shows a spot with which the artist has fallen in love."

The girl walking along the riverbank is probably Sisley's daughter, Jeanne.

THE SMALL MEADOWS
IN SPRING
About 1880-1
Alfred Sisley

Pissarro painted this when he was staying in south London. He painted the landscape on the spot, and added the figures later in his studio.

Close up, you can just see a dark grey patch where he painted over the figure of a woman walking down the road.

THE AVENUE, SYDENHAM
1871
Camille Pissarro

Sisley painted this landscape very quickly, to capture the changing light. He has used a few quick brushstrokes to add the figures of fishermen, sitting on the riverbank.

THE BRIDGE AT SÈVRES
About 1877
Alfred Sisley

5

PLAYING WITH COLOR

The Impressionists used lots of strong, vivid colors
to make their paintings as fresh and bright as possible.

LAVACOURT UNDER SNOW
About 1878-81
Claude-Oscar Monet

Before the Impressionists, most artists used blacks
and grays to paint shadows. But Monet believed
there was no black in nature.

In this painting, he used
pinks and yellows to
show the sun shining
on the snow...

...and blues and
greens to create
the shadows.

Renoir used huge blobs of pure color to paint this
seascape. He squirted paint straight from the tube onto
the canvas to show the texture of the foamy waves.

MOULIN HUET BAY, GUERNSEY
About 1883
Pierre-Auguste Renoir

Monet painted
from his window
as crowds took
to the streets
to celebrate a
French national
holiday. The red,
white and blue
of the French
flags dominate
the painting.

THE RUE MONTORGUEIL, PARIS
30TH JUNE 1878
1878
Claude-Oscar Monet

Up close, you can see Renoir's
big, quick brushstrokes.

The Impressionists were interested in scientific theories about color, particularly 'complementary colors'. These are pairs of colors that look brighter when they're next to each other.

Orange and blue are complementary colors. Renoir's orange boat looks brighter because it is floating along a blue river.

The colors opposite each other on this color wheel are 'complementary colors'.

THE SKIFF
1875
Pierre-Auguste Renoir

Monet used bright splashes of red to paint the poppies in this green field. The red poppies look brighter because red and green are complementary colors.

Monet may have painted his wife and son twice in the painting on the left. You can see them in the foreground, and the pair of figures in the distance may be them, too.

Monet wanted to show the tall poplar trees against the bright blue of the sky, so he painted this scene from a boat on the river.

THE POPPY FIELDS, NEAR ARGENTEUIL
1873
Claude-Oscar Monet

POPLARS ON THE EPTE
1891
Claude-Oscar Monet

BOATING AND BATHING

The Impressionists often painted river and seaside scenes.
They were inspired by the way water reflected sunlight.

Monet loved painting on the water so much
that he built himself a floating studio boat.
He used it to row up and down the river Seine,
looking for interesting scenes to paint.

Monet would go to great
lengths to get the perfect
view. He sat on rocking
boats, climbed rickety
ladders and even dug
trenches for his
paintings to stand in.

MONET IN HIS FLOATING STUDIO
1874
Edouard Manet

This picture by Monet shows the fashionable
resort of La Grenouillère, west of Paris,
where he spent a summer painting.

Morisot used a sketchy style to make it look as though she'd painted
this quickly, on the spot. But although she painted the background
in the park, the models posed for her in her studio.

BATHERS AT LA GRENOUILLÈRE
1869
Claude-Oscar Monet

SUMMER'S DAY
About 1879
Berthe Morisot

Can you spot the swimmers
bobbing up and down
in the water?

Monet was inspired to paint outdoors by his friend, Eugène Boudin. Monet and Boudin went on trips to Trouville beach, in Normandy, and they both painted scenes there. Monet owned this painting by Boudin, which shows vacationers dressed in the latest fashions, with parasols to shade them from the sun.

BEACH SCENE, TROUVILLE
About 1870-4
Eugène Boudin

Monet painted this picture of his wife, Camille, soon after their wedding. It took just one sitting to paint. The woman in black is probably the wife of Monet's friend Boudin.

Monet painted this picture on the beach, and tiny grains of sand are trapped in the paint.

THE BEACH
AT TROUVILLE
1870
Claude-Oscar Monet

Degas didn't like painting outdoors. He said that looking at too many coastal scenes made him feel 'drafty'. He made this beach scene using a model in his studio.

If you look closely, you can see that the smoke from the boats in the background is blowing in different directions — but in real life, the wind would blow the smoke in only one direction.

BEACH SCENE
About 1869-70
Hilaire-Germain-Edgar Degas

RENOIR'S PEOPLE

"Why shouldn't art be pretty?" Renoir said. "There are enough unpleasant things in the world." He loved painting beautiful women and sunlit scenes.

This painting is of Renoir's friend, a socialite and piano player named Misia Sert. She was famous for her beauty, so artists often wanted to paint her.

Renoir painted this at a popular riverside restaurant outside Paris. He ate there a lot, and often paid for his meals with paintings. Most of the people in this painting were his friends. The men wearing vests have just been rowing along the river.

MISIA SERT
1904
Pierre-Auguste Renoir

This is Aline — Renoir's girlfriend, who later became his wife.

LUNCHEON OF THE BOATING PARTY
1881
Pierre-Auguste Renoir

There are six different kinds of hats in this painting...

cap

cloche

bowler hat

top hat

bell hat

straw boating hat

The man in the straw hat is an artist called Gustave Caillebotte. He exhibited his work with the Impressionists and bought lots of their paintings.

This painting shows Renoir's friends enjoying themselves on a Sunday afternoon at an outdoor dance in Paris. They dressed up in their best clothes to be painted.

Norbert and Georges were two friends of Renoir's.

DANCE AT LE MOULIN DE LA GALETTE
1876
Pierre-Auguste Renoir

This painting is so large that the people are almost life-size. A friend of Renoir's claimed that Renoir carried the huge canvas to the dance hall every day and painted it all on the spot.

Renoir painted these dancing girls to hang in a wealthy Parisian's dining room. He used the same model for both paintings, but the head of the girl with castanets was modeled on his maid, Gabrielle Renard. Gabrielle worked for his family for years and appears in many of his paintings.

This photo shows Gabrielle surrounded by Renoir's paintings.

When Renoir was old and sick, Gabrielle looked after him. When Renoir found it hard to hold his paintbrush, she tied it to his hand.

DANCING GIRL
WITH TAMBOURINE
1909
Pierre-Auguste Renoir

DANCING GIRL
WITH CASTANETS
1909
Pierre-Auguste Renoir

MONET'S GARDEN

Monet once said, "Perhaps I owe having become a painter to flowers." He spent over twenty years creating a beautiful garden at his house in Giverny, east of Paris, to inspire his art.

Monet painted lots of huge canvases showing the waterlilies floating in his pond. He wanted to make his paintings so big that the viewer would be drawn into them.

Monet dabbed delicate pink and white flowers on green lily pads.

WATER-LILIES
After 1916
Claude-Oscar Monet

This was painted at sunset. Monet often painted the same scene at different times of day, to capture the different effects of light.

Here are some of the rough pencil sketches Monet made before he started painting in color.

WATER-LILIES, SETTING SUN
About 1907
Claude-Oscar Monet

This is a photo of
Monet in his garden.

Monet used
lots of fresh
greens in
this painting
to show his
Japanese
bridge on
a summer's
morning.

Monet owned a print of a Japanese
bridge. He liked it so much that he
built one just like it in his garden,
and he painted it over and over again.

THE WATER-LILY POND
1899
Claude-Oscar Monet

The view from the back door of Monet's house
looked out along this broad path. In summer, it was
overgrown with colorful flowers.

Monet probably painted these irises
looking down from his Japanese bridge.

PATH IN MONET'S GARDEN, GIVERNY
1902
Claude-Oscar Monet

Lots of bright flowers hang down
from above the path.

IRISES
About 1914-17
Claude-Oscar Monet

13

DRESSING UP

Renoir and Monet paid close attention to the clothes people wore. They were inspired by painting the rich colors and delicate textures of pretty fabrics.

This city scene shows a crowd of people in fashionable clothes.

Renoir repainted the woman on the left a few years after he'd finished the painting.

This x-ray shows what she used to look like. She was originally wearing a bonnet, but by the time Renoir repainted her, the fashions had changed. He painted out the bonnet and gave her a simple dress.

THE UMBRELLAS
About 1881-6
Pierre-Auguste Renoir

Renoir made lots of sketches of clothes, so that he could add accurate details to this painting, such as the shiny buttons on these shoes.

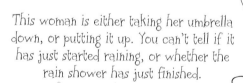

This woman is either taking her umbrella down, or putting it up. You can't tell if it has just started raining, or whether the rain shower has just finished.

Renoir changed his painting style while he was working on *The Umbrellas*. He repainted the woman on the left in his new style. His brushstrokes are smoother and more definite.

The dazzling white dresses in this painting stand out vividly against the green garden. Women often wore corsets under their dresses to make their waists look tiny, and hooped skirts to make their dresses stick out.

This page from a magazine shows the latest fashions in hats in 1873.

WOMEN IN A GARDEN
About 1866
Claude-Oscar Monet

The woman on the swing is wearing a dress covered in blue bows. Renoir made each bow look slightly different. The three figures on the left are all wearing straw hats to shade them from the sun.

Monet painted this eight years after the painting above. His style had become much more sketchy. This woman is sitting in the shade, so she doesn't need her parasol to shield her from the sun.

The little girl is wearing a cotton pinafore over her clothes, so they don't get dirty.

THE SWING
1876
Pierre-Auguste Renoir

WOMAN SEATED ON A BENCH
1874
Claude-Oscar Monet

PAINTING THE CITY

In the 19th century, cities were bigger and busier than ever before.
Many Impressionist paintings capture the excitement of city life.

THE BOULEVARD MONTMARTRE AT NIGHT
1897
Camille Pissarro

Pissarro painted this bustling night scene from his hotel window. He used blurry brush strokes to show the way light reflected off the wet street.

Up close, the carriages, streetlights and shops just look like splotches of paint.

From the 1850s onwards, Paris was completely transformed. The Emperor Napoleon III commissioned architects to modernize the city, building grand, straight avenues and new public parks. Caillebotte's painting shows off the impressive new streets and buildings.

The figures are cut off by the edges of the painting, which makes it feel as though you could step into the scene — or one of the people could step out.

PARIS STREET; RAINY DAY
1877
Gustave Caillebotte

Monet wanted to paint a smoky, blurry picture, so he decided to paint the smokiest place he could think of — a railway station.

He persuaded the director of this station in Paris to stop the trains while he made this painting. He even got the train drivers to cram their engines with coal, so there was lots of smoke rushing out of the funnels for him to paint.

THE GARE ST-LAZARE
1877
Claude-Oscar Monet

This view across the River Thames was probably painted from a window at the Savoy Hotel, where Monet was staying. He painted more than a hundred oil paintings of the river during his visits to London.

The fiery colors of the sunset are reflected in the river.

Monet painted this misty scene of the Thames when he was staying in London. He said he enjoyed painting London in the mist, because it hid all the ugly parts of the city.

PARLIAMENT, SUNSET
1904
Claude-Oscar Monet

THE THAMES BELOW WESTMINSTER
About 1871
Claude-Oscar Monet

Showtime

19th century Paris was a spectacular place at night.
There were concerts, ballets and circuses to see. The Impressionists
didn't just paint the shows — they painted the audiences, too.

Degas wanted to show a famous circus performer
called Miss La La from below — so you feel as if
you're in the audience. Here she is hanging
from a rope by her teeth.

Manet took nearly a year to paint this scene of the Folies-Bergère,
a famous club in Paris. In the mirror behind the bar, you can see
the audience watching an acrobatic show.

MISS LA LA AT
THE CIRQUE FERNANDO
1879
Hilaire-Germain-Edgar Degas

A BAR AT THE
FOLIES-BERGÈRE
1882
Edouard Manet

Manet signed his painting in an
unusual way. He wrote his name
on the label of a beer bottle.

This woman is watching
the show through a pair
of opera glasses.

The legs of a trapeze artist
are just visible in the top left
corner of the painting.

Manet painted this during a concert, but he's more interested in the waitress than the dancer in the background.

The dancer is out of focus, as if she's in a photograph.

A friend of Degas's, a bassoonist named Désiré Dihau, asked him to paint his portrait. Degas placed him in the middle of the orchestra, with his fellow musicians.

CORNER OF A CAFÉ-CONCERT
Probably 1878-80
Edouard Manet

THE ORCHESTRA AT THE OPERA
About 1870
Hilaire-Germain-Edgar Degas

Here, Renoir shows a young girl on a trip to the theatre. She's leaning forward to see the stage, but all we can see is the audience.

The girl behind is using binoculars to get a better view.

AT THE THEATRE
(LA PREMIÈRE SORTIE)
1876-7
Pierre-Auguste Renoir

Renoir uses dashes of bright color to paint the ribbon on the girl's hat.

Degas's Dancers

Degas became famous for his paintings of ballerinas. He spent hours drawing dancers behind the scenes at the Paris Opera House.

Degas was more interested in what was going on behind the scenes than the ballet itself. He painted young dancers practicing their moves.

Degas's paintings shocked people, because they showed how hard it was to be a dancer. The dancers were often young girls, who had to work very long, tiring hours.

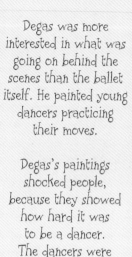

Degas did hundreds of drawings to get his figures just right, before he started painting.

Degas didn't just draw ballet dancers — he drew Russian dancers, too. He smudged his pastels to show how fast they are dancing.

BALLET DANCERS
About 1890-1900
Hilaire-Germain-Edgar Degas

RUSSIAN DANCERS
About 1899
Hilaire-Germain-Edgar Degas

Photography had recently been invented, and it influenced Degas's work. The dancer in blue has been cut off by the edge of the picture, as if this were a photo rather than a painting.

These pictures look as if they've been painted very quickly - but Degas actually spent hours placing his figures just where he wanted them.

FOUR BALLERINAS ON THE STAGE
About 1896
Hilaire-Germain-Edgar Degas

This picture shows a dancing class, led by dancing teacher Jules Perrot. One of the dancers is showing her moves to the teacher.

The other dancers look tired and bored, while a little dog peeks out from behind the legs of one of the dancers.

Jules Perrot was a famous dancing teacher. He had once been a ballet dancer himself.

THE BALLET CLASS
About 1871–1874
Hilaire-Germain-Edgar Degas

This dancer was the only sculpture Degas exhibited in his lifetime. He made it in wax, and then added real clothes, ballet shoes, a hair ribbon and hair (actually a horsehair wig). The wax was tinted to be the color of skin... and the effect was so real, it frightened people.

This photo shows a copy of the sculpture, cast in bronze after Degas died.

Degas used soft pastels to show the stage lights shining on this ballerina. It makes you feel as though you're looking down at the stage from a box, and the dancer seems to be smiling right at you.

LITTLE DANCER
AGED FOURTEEN
1880–1, cast about 1922
Hilaire-Germain-
Edgar Degas

THE STAR, OR DANCER ON THE STAGE
About 1876–77
Hilaire-Germain-Edgar Degas

21

FRIENDS AND FAMILY

The Impressionists didn't have to go far from home to find inspiration for their paintings. They often painted their families and friends.

PORTRAIT OF MONSIEUR
AND MADAME EDOUARD MANET
About 1868-69
Hilaire-Germain-Edgar Degas

This relaxed portrait of Manet and his wife was painted by Degas, who gave it to Manet as a present. But Manet thought Degas had made his wife look ugly — so he chopped off the side of the painting to hide her face.

Renoir was friendly with a family named the Charpentiers. They helped Renoir by lending him rooms to hold exhibitions in. In return he painted this portrait of Madame Charpentier and her children.

Bazille was a talented young painter, who was friends with Renoir and many of the other Impressionists. But when war broke out between France and Prussia, he became a soldier. "I don't intend to die, because there's too much I want to do with my life", he said, but he was killed soon afterwards.

PORTRAIT OF RENOIR
1867
Frédéric Bazille

MADAME CHARPENTIER
WITH HER CHILDREN
About 1878
Pierre-Auguste Renoir

Degas visited Italy, to study Italian paintings.
He painted his cousin Elena while he was there.

This is a portrait
of Camille
Pissarro's son,
Félix, age seven.
When Félix grew
up, he became
an artist, too,
but he died when
he was just 24.

PORTRAIT OF ELENA CARAFA
About 1875
Hilaire-Germain-Edgar Degas

FÉLIX PISSARRO
1881
Camille Pissarro

This is a portrait of
Hélène, the daughter
of one of Degas's
friends, Henri Rouart.
But the painting is
really more about
Henri than about
his daughter —
she's surrounded
by his impressive
art collection.

As well as painting his friends,
Degas liked taking photographs
of them. Here, a family named the
Halévys are posed around him,
pretending to be angels.

HÉLÈNE ROUART IN HER
FATHER'S STUDY
About 1886
Hilaire-Germain-Edgar Degas

THE APOTHEOSIS OF DEGAS
About 1886
Taken by Walter Barnes,
composed by Degas

You can see an ancient Egyptian
figure in the glass cabinet in the background.

In the middle, Degas is about to rise
up to heaven. Degas sent this photograph
to all his friends as a joke.

DAILY LIFE

In the 19th century, art usually showed important people and grand occasions. The Impressionists shocked people by showing paintings of ordinary people doing ordinary things.

This rich, warm painting shows a girl holding her hair, as her maid combs it.

Because neither of the people in the picture are looking at the viewer, it's as if they don't realize that anyone can see them. Degas said he wanted his paintings to be like "looking through a keyhole."

The girl's hair is the same color as the room around her.

COMBING THE HAIR
About 1896
Hilaire-Germain-Edgar Degas

This is Berthe Morisot's most famous painting. It shows Berthe's sister Edma watching tenderly over her daughter Blanche. Morisot showed this painting in the first Impressionist exhibition.

At the time, lots of art critics thought that women who worked in a laundry weren't a proper subject for painting, but Degas ignored them. He spent lots of time sketching laundresses, and made pictures of them from memory. These laundresses look exhausted, showing what long hours they had to work.

Shhhh!

THE CRADLE
1872
Berthe Morisot

WOMEN IRONING
About 1884-1886
Hilaire-Germain-Edgar Degas

Pissarro originally called this picture *The Goose Girl*. You can see some geese in the background.

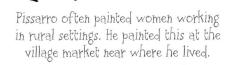

Pissarro often painted women working in rural settings. He painted this at the village market near where he lived.

A WOOL-CARDER
1880
Camille Pissarro

THE PORK BUTCHER
1883
Camille Pissarro

The woman isn't really a pork butcher. Pissarro's niece, Nini, posed for the painting.

Pissarro was inspired by Italian artists who painted straight on to walls. Instead of using a canvas, he decided to paint this picture on concrete. Unfortunately it was broken twice. Close up, you can still see the cracks where it has been repaired.

Degas wanted the people in his pictures to look as natural as possible, so he often went to cafés and sketched the people he saw there. These two men are reading a newspaper. One of them has a magnifying glass, and the other is wearing a monocle — a single eye glass.

AT THE CAFÉ CHÂTEAUDUN
About 1869-71
Hilaire-Germain-Edgar Degas

25

Pissarro was the only artist who showed his paintings in all eight of the Impressionist exhibitions. His paintings inspired lots of other artists, including Monet, Degas and Cézanne.

Pissarro painted this sunny landscape near Louveciennes, to the west of Paris, where his friends Monet and Renoir also painted. Soon after he finished this painting, in 1870, war broke out between France and Prussia. Pissarro and his family moved to England to keep safe.

When he got back to France, Pissarro discovered that almost all of the paintings he'd left behind had been destroyed. Prussian soldiers had turned his house into a slaughterhouse and used the paintings as aprons.

THE VIEW FROM LOUVECIENNES
1869–70
Camille Pissarro

This painting shows Pissarro's son Rodo sitting at the table, while a maid sweeps the floor. One of Pissarro's pictures is hanging on the wall.

Pissarro painted this peaceful winter scene in Fox Hill, south London, where he lived during the war between France and Prussia.

THE LITTLE COUNTRY MAID
1882
Camille Pissarro

FOX HILL, UPPER NORWOOD
1870
Camille Pissarro

When he got older, Pissarro often painted street scenes in Paris. This painting shows the view from his studio window.

Pissarro painted the horses and carriages rattling along...

...and people hurrying down the wet street.

THE PONT-NEUF,
AFTERNOON OF RAIN
1901
Camille Pissarro

Pissarro painted himself over and over again, at different stages in his life. This is Pissarro's last self-portrait, which he painted in 1903.

Pissarro died the year he painted this self portrait. He painted 57 paintings that year, and sold two of them to the most important museum in Paris - the Louvre.

SELF PORTRAIT
1903
Camille Pissarro

This photograph shows Pissarro working in his studio beside the Pont Neuf.

IMPRESSIONIST PARIS

The Impressionists first met, studied art and exhibited their paintings in Paris. But they also traveled further afield, to paint the outdoors and relax in the countryside.

The Impressionists held their first exhibition in this house in Paris, which belonged to their friend, a photographer named Nadar. It was on the Boulevard des Capucines.

Monet showed this painting of the street in the first Impressionist exhibition.

BOULEVARD DES CAPUCINES
1873-4
Claude-Oscar Monet

Manet and a group of his friends often met at a café called the Café Guerbois to discuss ideas about art.

Sometimes their discussions turned into arguments. Once, Manet argued with his friend Duranty about a review of one of his paintings, and challenged him to a duel. Luckily, they both survived.

A STUDIO IN THE BATIGNOLLES
1870
Henri Fantin-Latour

Émile Zola, a writer

Claude-Oscar Monet

Pierre-Auguste Renoir

This painting shows Manet seated at his easel, surrounded by his friends, at a studio in the Batignolles, an area of Paris.

Edouard Manet

Frédéric Bazille

This is an advertisement for the famous Folies-Bergère nightclub. Lots of the Impressionists went there to enjoy concerts and acrobatic shows.

THÉÂTRE DE L'OPÉRA

Samedi 30 Janvier
1ᵉʳ GRAND BAL MASQUÉ

Degas and Renoir often painted the dancers and the audience at the Paris Opera House.

This photograph shows Monet painting one of his enormous waterlily paintings at his studio in Giverny, northwest of Paris.

La Grenouillère was a fashionable resort just outside Paris, where people often went on Sundays, to swim in the river and dance long into the night. Renoir and Monet made lots of paintings there.

BAL DE LA GRENOUILLÈRE

TOUS LES JEUDIS

This is Monet's palette.

La Grenouillère means 'frogpond'.

29

LASTING IMPRESSIONS

The Impressionists inspired other artists to break the rules and try out new ideas. Painting was never the same again.

Vincent van Gogh used bright, pure colors and thick brushstrokes, like the Impressionists.

But van Gogh didn't just use colors to make his paintings bright. He used them to show his feelings. For him, yellow represented joy. He painted this picture of sunflowers when he was very happy.

SUNFLOWERS
1888
Vincent van Gogh

Van Gogh painted this chair as a kind of self portrait. It represents what he thought of himself. He chose an ordinary kitchen chair, because he saw himself as an ordinary person.

VAN GOGH'S CHAIR
1888
Vincent van Gogh

Van Gogh included these sprouting onions in his picture as a sign of new life. He had been through a sad time, but he hoped that things were soon going to get better.

Georges Seurat painted scenes of ordinary city life, as many of the Impressionists did, but he used a less sketchy style and he painted on a grand scale — this painting is 3 meters (nearly 10 feet) wide. Eventually he developed a new style of painting called 'pointillism', creating images out of lots and lots of tiny dots.

He went back and added dots to part of this painting — if you look closely, you can see blue dots on the boy's red hat, for example.

BATHERS AT ASNIÈRES
1884
Georges Seurat

Like the Impressionists, Rousseau used thick paint and vivid colors, but his style was very different than theirs. While the Impressionists observed nature, Rousseau invented landscapes from his imagination.

SURPRISED!
1891
Henri Rousseau

Rousseau probably went to the zoo to draw this tiger.

Rousseau's tiger looks scary, but it also looks as though it's scared of whatever it's seen.

Paul Cézanne was a friend of many of the Impressionists, and they inspired him to paint outdoors in the countryside. He used blocks of different colors to give depth to his paintings.

HILLSIDE IN PROVENCE
About 1890–92
Paul Cézanne

Degas inspired the younger artist, Toulouse-Lautrec, to paint vibrant, glamorous scenes of Paris night life. He made lots of posters to advertise different shows and theatres in the city.

Troupe de Mlle ÉGLANTINE
Eglantine   Cléopatre
Jane Avril   Gazelle

LA TROUPE DE
MADEMOISELLE EGLANTINE
1896
Henri de Toulouse-Lautrec

ACKNOWLEDGEMENTS

Pages 2-3: Self Portrait with a Beret by Monet, (private collection) Photo © Lefevre Fine Art Ltd., London / Bridgeman. Impression, Sunrise by Monet (Musée Marmottan, Paris) © Musée Marmottan, Paris, France / Giraudon / Bridgeman. Self Portrait by Camille Pissarro (Musée d'Orsay, Paris) © The Gallery Collection / Corbis. Self Portrait by Renoir (Sterling & Francine Clark Art Institute, Williamstown, USA) © Sterling & Francine Clark Art Institute, Williamstown, USA/ Bridgeman. Music in the Tuileries Gardens (detail) by Manet (National Gallery, London) © The National Gallery, London. Berthe Morisot with a Bouquet of Violets by Manet (Musée d'Orsay, Paris) © Musée d'Orsay, Paris, France / Bridgeman. Self Portrait by Degas (Museu Calouste Gulbenkian, Lisbon, Portugal) © Museu Calouste Gulbenkian, Lisbon, Portugal / Giraudon / Bridgeman. Self Portrait by Cassatt (Smithsonian Institution, USA) © Smithsonian Institution / Corbis. Pages 4-5: Snow Scene at Argenteuil by Monet (National Gallery, London) © The National Gallery, London. Grainstack, Sunset by Monet (Museum of Fine Arts, Boston, USA) © Bettmann / Corbis. The Louvre Under Snow by Camille Pissarro (National Gallery, London) © The National Gallery, London. The Small Meadows in Spring by Sisley (National Gallery, London, on loan from Tate) © Tate, London, 2010. The Avenue, Sydenham by Camille Pissarro (National Gallery, London) © The National Gallery, London. The Bridge at Sevres by Sisley (National Gallery, London, on loan from Tate) © Tate, London, 2010. Pages 6-7: Lavacourt Under Snow, by Monet (National Gallery, London) © The National Gallery, London. The Rue Montorgueil, Paris, 30th June 1878, by Monet (Musée d'Orsay, Paris) © Musée d'Orsay, Paris, France / Giraudon / Bridgeman. Moulin Huet Bay, Guernsey, by Renoir (National Gallery, London) © The National Gallery, London. The Skiff by Renoir (National Gallery, London) © The National Gallery, London. The Poppy Fields, Near Argenteuil by Monet (Musée d'Orsay, Paris) © The Gallery Collection / Corbis. Poplars on the Epte by Monet (National Gallery London, on loan from Tate) © Tate, London, 2010. Pages 8-9: Monet in his Floating Studio by Manet (Neue Pinakothek, Munich) © Neue Pinakothek, Munich, Germany / Bridgeman. Bathers at La Grenouillère by Monet (National Gallery, London) © The National Gallery, London. Summer's Day by Morisot (National Gallery, London) © The National Gallery, London. Beach Scene, Trouville by Boudin (National Gallery, London) © The National Gallery, London. The Beach at Trouville by Monet (National Gallery, London) © The National Gallery, London. Beach Scene by Degas (National Gallery, London) © The National Gallery, London. Pages 10-11: Misia Sert by Renoir (National Gallery, London) © The National Gallery, London. Luncheon of the Boating Party by Renoir (The Phillips Collection, Washington DC, USA) © Phillips Collection, Washington DC, USA / Bridgeman. Le Dance at the Moulin de la Galette by Renoir (Musée d'Orsay, Paris) © Musée d'Orsay, Paris, France / Giraudon / Bridgeman. Portrait of Gabrielle Renard (Musée Marmottan, Paris) Musée Marmottan, Paris, France / Giraudon / Bridgeman. Dancing Girl with Castanets by Renoir (National Gallery, London) © The National Gallery, London. Dancing Girl with Tambourine by Renoir (National Gallery, London) © The National Gallery, London. Pages 12-13: Water-Lilies by Monet (National Gallery, London) © The National Gallery, London. Pond with Water-Lilies, purple pencil on paper by Monet (Musée Marmottan, Paris) © Musée Marmottan, Paris, France / Giraudon / Bridgeman. Water-Lilies, Setting Sun by Monet (National Gallery, London) © The National Gallery, London. Claude Monet in Front of his Bridge in Giverny (Musée d'Orsay, Paris) © Musée d'Orsay / Dist. RMN / Patrice Schmidt. The Water-Lily Pond by Monet (National Gallery, London) © The National Gallery, London. Path in Monet's Garden, Giverny, by Monet (Belvedere Gallery, Vienna) © The Gallery Collection/Corbis. Irises by Monet (National Gallery, London) © The National Gallery, London. Pages 14-15: The Umbrellas by Renoir (National Gallery, London) © The National Gallery, London. Parisian Bonnets © Getty Images. Women in a Garden by Monet (Musée d'Orsay, Paris) © Musée d'Orsay, Paris, France / Giraudon / Bridgeman. The Swing by Renoir (Musée d'Orsay, Paris) © Musée d'Orsay, Paris, France / Giraudon / Bridgeman. Woman Seated on a Bench by Monet (The National Gallery, London, on loan from Tate) © Tate, London, 2010. Pages 16-17: The Boulevard Montmartre at Night by Camille Pissarro (National Gallery, London) © The National Gallery, London. Paris Street; Rainy Day by Caillebotte (The Art Institute of Chicago, USA) © Burstein Collection / Corbis. The Gare St-Lazare by Monet (National Gallery, London) © The National Gallery, London. Parliament, Sunset by Monet (Kunsthaus, Zurich) © Christie's Images / Corbis. The Thames Below Westminster by Monet (National Gallery, London) © The National Gallery, London. Pages 18-19: Miss La La at the Cirque Fernando by Degas (National Gallery, London) © The National Gallery, London. A Bar at the Folies-Bergère by Manet (Courtauld Institute of Art Gallery, London) © Samuel Courtauld Trust, Courtauld Institute of Art Gallery, London / Bridgeman. Corner of a Café-Concert by Manet (National Gallery, London) © The National Gallery, London. The Orchestra at the Opera by Degas (Musée d'Orsay) © Musée d'Orsay, Paris, France / Giraudon / Bridgeman. At the Theatre (La Première Sortie) by Renoir (National Gallery, London) © The National Gallery, London. Pages 20-21: Ballet Dancers by Degas (National Gallery, London) © The National Gallery, London. Russian Dancers by Degas (National Gallery, London) © The National Gallery, London. Four Ballerinas on the Stage by Degas (Museum of Art, Sao Paolo, Brazil) © The Gallery Collection / Corbis. The Ballet Class by Degas (Musée d'Orsay, Paris) © The Gallery Collection / Corbis. Little Dancer Aged Fourteen by Degas (Tate Gallery, London) © Tate, London, 2010. The Star or Dancer on the Stage by Degas (Musée d'Orsay, Paris) © The Gallery Collection/Corbis. Pages 22-23: Portrait of Monsieur and Madame Edouard Manet by Degas (Municipal Museum of Art, Kitakyushu, Japan) © The Gallery Collection / Corbis. Portrait of Renoir by Bazille (Musée d'Orsay, Paris) © The Gallery Collection/Corbis. Madame Charpentier with her Children by Renoir (Metropolitan Museum of Art, New York, USA) © Bridgeman. Portrait of Elena Carafa by Degas (National Gallery, London) © The National Gallery, London. Portrait of Félix Pissarro by Camille Pissarro (National Gallery London, on loan from Tate) © Tate, London, 2010. Hélène Rouart in Her Father's Study by Degas (National Gallery, London) © The National Gallery, London. The Apotheosis of Degas by Degas and Walter Barnes (Musée d'Orsay) © RMN (Musée d'Orsay) / Hervé Lewandowski. Pages 24-25: Combing the Hair by Degas (National Gallery, London) © The National Gallery, London. The Cradle by Morisot (Musée d'Orsay) © The Gallery Collection / Corbis. Women Ironing by Degas (Musée d'Orsay) © France / Giraudon / Bridgeman. A Wool-Carder by Camille Pissarro (National Gallery, London, on loan from Tate) © Tate, London, 2010. The Pork Butcher by Camille Pissarro (National Gallery, London, on loan from Tate) © Tate, London, 2010. At the Café Châteaudun by Degas (National Gallery, London) © The National Gallery, London. Pages 26-27: View from Louveciennes by Camille Pissarro (National Gallery, London) © The National Gallery, London. The Little Country Maid by Camille Pissarro (The National Gallery, London, on loan from Tate) © Tate, London, 2010. Fox Hill, Upper Norwood by Camille Pissarro (National Gallery, London) © The National Gallery, London. The Pont-Neuf, Afternoon of Rain by Camille Pissarro (Private collection) © Christie's Images / Corbis. Self Portrait by Camille Pissarro (Tate, London) © Tate, London, 2010. Camille Pissarro in his Studio (Private Collection) © Roger Viollet/Getty Images. Pages 28-29: Photograph of the Studio of Nadar by Nadar (Private Collection) © Archives Charmet. Boulevard des Capucines by Monet (The Nelson-Atkins Museum of Art, Kansas City, USA) © Boltin Picture Library / Bridgeman. A Studio in the Batignolles by Fantin-Latour (Musée d'Orsay, Paris) © Musée d'Orsay, Paris, France/ Giraudon/ Bridgeman. La Belle Otero at the Folies-Bergères © Private Collection / Bridgeman. Reproduction of a poster advertising the first 'Grand Bal Masque', Theatre de L'Opera, Paris © Private Collection / The Stapleton Collection/ Bridgeman. Monet in his Studio © Private Collection / Roger-Viollet, Paris / Bridgeman. La Grenouillère advert © Private Collection / Archives Charmet / Bridgeman. Pages 30-31: Sunflowers by Van Gogh (National Gallery, London) © The National Gallery, London. Van Gogh's Chair by Van Gogh (National Gallery, London) © The National Gallery, London. Bathers at Asnières by Seurat (National Gallery, London) © The National Gallery, London. Surprised! by Rousseau (National Gallery, London) © The National Gallery, London. Hillside in Provence by Cézanne (National Gallery, London) © The National Gallery, London. The Troupe of Mademoiselle Eglantine by Toulouse-Lautrec (San Diego Museum of Art, USA) © San Diego Museum of Art, USA / Gift of the Baldwin M. Baldwin Foundation / Bridgeman.

Picture research by Ruth King and Sam Noonan

First published in 2010 by Usborne Publishing Ltd,
Usborne House, 83-85 Saffron Hill, London EC1N 8RT, England.
www.usborne.com Copyright © 2010 Usborne Publishing Ltd.

WHO WERE THE IMPRESSIONISTS?

PAINTING
OUTDOORS

PAGES 2-3

PAGES 4-5

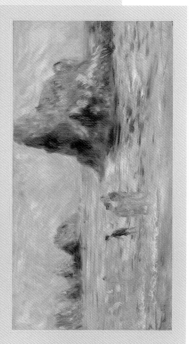

PAGES 6-7

Boating and Bathing

Pages 8-9

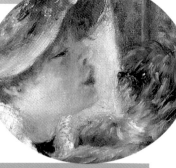

Renoir's People

Pages 10-11

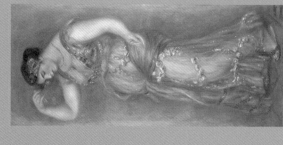

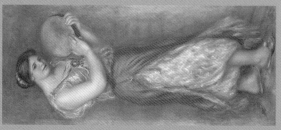

DRESSING UP

PAGES 14-15

PAGES 16-17

PAINTING THE CITY

PAGES 18-19

Degas's Dancers

PAGES 20-21

FRIENDS AND FAMILY

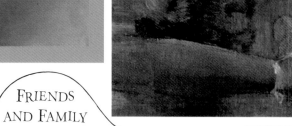

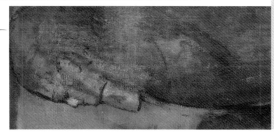

DAILY LIFE

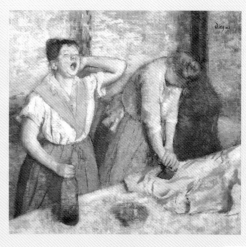

PAGES 24-25

PAGES 22-23

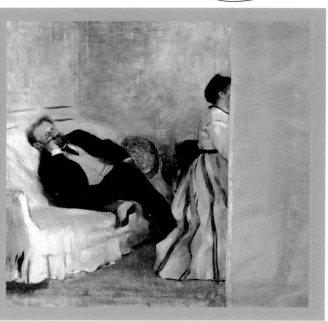

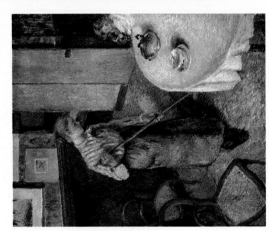

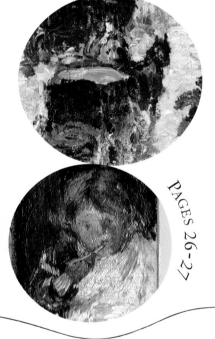

PAGES 26-27

IMPRESSIONIST
PARIS

BAL DE LA GRENOUILLÈRE

TOUS LES JEUDIS

RETOUR
Onze heures 21

GARE S.T LAZARE
LIGNE DE S.T GERMAIN
STATION : CHATOU-CROISSY

V. PALYART & FILS

89. F.BG S.T Denis, PARIS

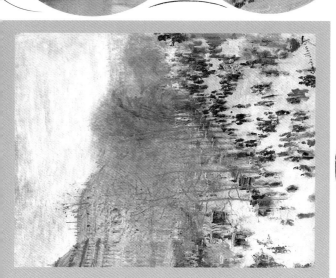

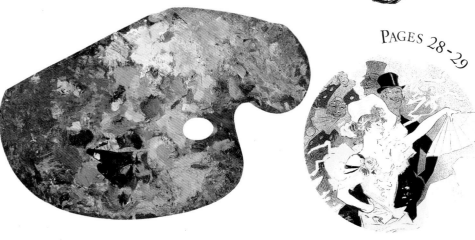

PAGES 28-29